This book belongs to

_____

Poppy
the
Pooting Panda

By Humor Heals Us

My name is Poppy the Pooting Panda.
I like to think I'm pretty smart.
Though every time I try to eat,
I poot and toot and **fart**.

I love bamboo shoots.
It is my favorite **food**.
But pooting while you're eating
Is often seen as rude.

I try hard not to do it,
And hold my pooting in.
But every time I take a bite,
My farts would start again.

"I wish you could control it,"
My panda dad would say.
"It's really quite embarrassing,
You do it **every** day!"

This made me feel quite sad,
It isn't fun to poot
Up to 40 times a day,
And sometimes more to boot!

Perhaps it's just the bamboo shoots
That make me fart and toot.
I thought one day,
Maybe I'll try the **roots**.

So, I tried to change my diet,
But my farts were not relieved.
I'm not sure what else I can do.
I guess I'll try the **leaves**.

At first, it seemed to work,
My pooting seemed to slow.
But when I thought I had been cured,
My farts still appeared to blow.

I pooted powerfully,
And I tooted hard and long.
I even farted to the tune
Of my favorite song.

Sometimes I don't eat
To make my pooting stop.
But that just makes me hungrier
And I then I go *pop...pop...pop!*

Many pandas thought I was fun.
To them, farting was cool.
But in front of some panda friends,
I felt like a pooting **fool**.

"Do other creatures poot this much?"
Is a question I asked.
"No, nothing farts as much as **you**,"
My mother said, aghast.

I just can't help it.
I've tried so hard to cease.
I don't know what else I can do
To make this pooting **ease**.

When eating bamboo shoots one day,
I thought I'd climb a tree.
That way I'd not stink others out,
And be fart and **poot-free.**

But that plan didn't work so well,
When I farted there was **chatter**.
My pooting was so awful,
It made all the monkeys scatter.

One day some nasty hunters came
To steal pandas for their zoo.
They tried to capture me,
But that wasn't wise to do.

The other pandas tried to flee,
But they weren't safe yet.
For even though they climbed up trees,
The men had traps and nets.

I turned my back on them
As soon as they got **close**.
I farted such a dreadful smell,
It made them grab their nose.

I may have chased the hunters
With my powerful poots that day,
But I'll be ready to do it again,
And keep them far away.

Now I'm seen as a hero,
No one speaks about my farts.
It doesn't matter that I smell,
There's bravery in my heart.

Follow us on FB and IG @humorhealsus
To vote on new title names and freebies, visit
us at humorhealsus.com for more information.

 @humorhealsus   @humorhealsus